RELATIONSH

THE IDEAL COUPLE

What Every Healthy Relationship Needs To Have In Order To Thrive

Christy Horton

Table of Contents

Chapter 1:

10 Ways To Build A Strong Relationship

Relationships are not always easy, especially when both people aren't exactly on the same page. But the key to a strong and healthy relationship doesn't necessarily mean you guys are mirror images of each other when it comes to your opinions and personality. Understanding and adaptability is the key to a successful relationship.

When it comes down to the two people involved, no two relationships are the same. As we are unique individuals, so will our relationships be as well. The needs, goals, perceptions, and growth vary from couple to couple. With that in mind, we are going to talk about the 10 signs that point to a strong relationship that all couples should strive for at some point in their time together.

1. Trust.

The foundation of any relationship is very much dependent on trust. More than love, trust is more important for the bond to be strong. Trust includes honesty, integrity, and at the same time feeling safe and comfortable with the person that you are with.

Trust has to be earned over time, by proving to your partner that they can count on you to be faithful in the relationship and also to be honest with things that are going on with your life.

Trust is also earned when you work with your partner in the same domain and you have a clear understanding of their passions.

2. Respect for personal space.

I feel that this needs to be heard loud and clear. Being in a relationship does not imply breathing down the neck of your partner all the time.

Doing so could potentially suffocate the other person and make the relationship bitter over time.

I am sure you don't like your personal space to be violated by someone else all the time, so expect the same adverse reactions if you do that to your partner as well.

It is very important that each individual in the relationship has the utmost respect for the other person's private space. Allowing room to breathe can be a wonderful way to recharge and come back to the relationship with renewed excitement and interest.

3. Spending quality time with your partner.

It is very important for two people in a relationship to spend quality time together. A certain time each week that you have set aside for your partner where the two of you will focus only on each other and nothing else. A time when you ask your partner the deep questions, to engage in insightful thought, or to simply be mindfully present in each other's company. It is an amazing feeling when your significant other engages you by asking about your day, asking how you are feeling, and making sure you are well taken care of.

While many thinks that quantity of time is important as well, I would argue that this could lead to complacency. It is important that you don't treat spending time with your partner by counting the hours, but by counting the moments instead.

4. Encouraging each other to achieve personal goals.

When your partner becomes your life coach who motivates you to become a better person every day and achieve your personal goals , this is where the bond grows beyond the surface level feelings into a much deeper emotional and spiritual connection.

By understanding the kind of service you need to provide to your partner to support their goals and dreams, you are in effect helping them achieve what they truly want in life. This proactiveness will make them fall in love with themselves and with you even more.

5. Physical Intimacy.

Physical intimacy doesn't necessarily imply sex. Sex is not necessary for a relationship to stick on provided both sides are on the same page. Even cuddles, hugs, and kissing your partner is an act of intimacy that is very important in any relationship. It is very crucial to have that understanding in the bedroom and to be able to openly express your needs, your desires, and your fantasies, and your inhibitions regarding physical intimacy with your partner. Lack of physical touch could result in loss of intimacy away from the bedroom. So be mindful that you keep that in check in your relationship.

6. Communication.

There is nothing more important than keeping the communication flowing with your partner. If you aren't comfortable in sharing your deepest emotions, fears, and insecurities with that person, you should probably think about why that is so. Your better half should not just be your partner in a relationship but should ideally by a very close and personal friend as well. There should not be inhibitions about expressing one's feelings and opinions about a matter out of fear that it might end up in a fight with the other person. Fights will inevitably happen in every relationship. How you manage the fights is what makes or breaks your strong bond.

7. Teamwork.

A relationship would become a burden if one person is constantly working hard to keep the other person comfortable and the other one doesn't contribute much. As the saying goes, team work makes the dream work. Be it household chores, cleaning the dishes, settling the bills, taking the dog out for a dump, both have to contribute equally for it to be a balanced relationship. Both will need to take the initiative to help out the other party where possible otherwise resentment and unhappiness might follow.

8. Personal Time.

This point overlaps quite a bit with providing personal space.

To be a more balanced individual, you really need to have that "me-time" for yourself. Time where you spend alone. Time where you engage in your favourite hobbies or sports that you might not share with your partner.

Giving yourself that "me-time" can also include having that favorite cup of coffee while watching your favorite shows, catching up with your friends, cooking your favorite meal, or watching your favorite team match. Once you start balancing time for yourself you start respecting your partner's personal space and time as well, and that gives the relationship a breath of fresh air and keeps you both going.

9. Talking to your partner, not to other people.

It is very easy in times of fights to simply run away from the problems you are facing and into your friends for shelter. While having a strong social support network is great to have, always ensure that you come back to the relationship with a clear mind and talk things through openly and without fear of judgement.

Miscommunications are usually high up on the list when it comes to disagreements. It is always best to sort out the differences there instead of running away and letting the situation escalate to an unresolvable point.

10. The 3 golden phrases.

Yes, you are right. In a relationship, you should be able to say 'I am sorry', 'Thank you', and 'I love you' as much as possible. Being able to express your love, regret, appreciativeness, and sorrow, will enlighten the bond between you and your partner. By verbally saying these words regularly, you are showing your partner that you can be vulnerable around them and that they can be the same with you.

A Strong relationship is not easy to build, but it is worth the effort if we take the time and effort to put into practice some of these points that we have discussed today. Take care and I'll see you in the next one.

Chapter 2:

<u>10 signs You're In A Healthy Relationship</u>

Good relationships are a prime ingredient for a happy life, and a bad one tends to be a miserable experience. We all know there's plenty of toxic relationships out there. We've seen them, and for many of us, we have been in them. According to a survey, a third of women and a quarter of men have experienced abusive relationships on average.

The term "perfect relationship" is nothing more than a myth. You don't just get one served on a plate. According to a therapist, "One thing healthy relationships largely share is adaptability. They adapt to circumstances because we can't escape the fact that we're always changing and going through different phases in life." It's not a secret that we all have our ups and downs and ebbs and flows, from time to time. And this may as well affect our relationship too. But one shouldn't strive for a perfect relationship; instead, endeavour to make the best one can.

Let's get to the heart of the matter: How do you know that you're in a healthy and robust relationship, or better stated: How do you know you're in a relationship that's good for you? These signs of a healthy relationship may be blazingly obvious, but sometimes we need things written in black and white for us to see that we're on the right path.

1. **<u>You both understand the need for personal space:</u>**

Healthy relationships are all about interdependence; that is, you rely on each other for mutual support but still maintain your identity as a unique individual. A famous saying goes, "Stand together, yet not too near together: For the pillars of the temple stand apart, And the oak tree and the cypress grow not in each other's shadow."

You don't wholly depend on your partner and know that you have a social circle outside of the relationship. Although you're always there for each other, you don't cling to your partner for every little need, and you spend your time pursuing your interests and hobbies too. Having your freedom in a relationship means that your partner should support your life outside the relationship and might not feel the need to know or be involved in every part of your life. And that means giving your partner the same freedom and independence. In other words, your relationship is balanced.

2. **<u>You can talk to each other about anything and everything:</u>**

They say that secrecy is the enemy of intimacy. And every healthy relationship is built on a foundation of honesty and trust. If you trust one another, you can be vulnerable and weak in their company because you recognize that instead of judging you, they will hold you and support you through the dark times. You're able to pour your heart out to them, no matter how stupid some things might sound. You don't keep secrets from each other. And when you're apart, you're not worried about them pursuing other people. You know they won't cheat or lie to you. You're safe and comfortable with them, knowing the fact that they won't ever hurt you, both physically or emotionally. You know they have your best interests in mind and respect you enough to encourage you to make your own choices. In conclusion, you respect each other's privacy, and the element of trust between you two comes naturally, and neither of you goes out of your way to work hard to "earn" their faith.

3. **You support and encourage each other's passions and ambitions:**

If your partner expresses his interest to become Batman, then you should assure that you'll hold the cape for him. If it's essential for them to, it should be important to you too, no matter how strange or bizarre their goals may sound. Even if you don't see eye to eye on something or have plans that aren't the same, healthy relationships are built on mutual inspiration and motivation; your partner should encourage you to be your best self, to face complex challenges, and to change the world, all by being there with you, supporting you through it all.

4. **You accept them for who they are:**

One of the most critical factors contributing to a healthy relationship is that you don't try to fix the other person. Love is all about seeing the flaws and blemishes of your partner and accepting them. It is about abiding by the bad habits and mannerisms of your significant other and working around them. It is about recognizing all the fears and insecurities and reassuring and comforting them. We all go through our bad days. We should strive to hold them in their bad days and dance and celebrate with them in their good ones. None of us are perfect; we're made with cracks and smudges, our souls have been shattered, and our skin is patchwork. There's nothing wrong with that. When your partner is broken, Vow to hold him together, and when your time comes, to be broken, beaten, restless, except that he'll keep you too.

5. Playfulness and Light-heartedness:

Healthy relationships are full of laughter and fun. It all comes down to joking and roasting each other playfully and laughing your hearts out. The spontaneity and adventures that you both might bring would eventually spice up your relationship. Sometimes one of you, or both of you, might feel emotionally or physically drained, or the challenges or distress might affect your relationship's tone. But being able to relieve the tension and share lighter moments, even briefly, strengthens your connection even in tough times.

6. Conflict Resolution:

Even in a healthy relationship, you'll have occasions where you might agree to disagree. It's entirely normal for couples to have disagreements and feel frustrated or angry with their partner. But that doesn't mean you should disrespect your partner based on his opinions and thinking. It all comes down to how you choose to address the conflict. You and your partner must talk about your differences politely, honestly, and with respect. Know when you or your partner is wrong, and apologize rightfully for it. You should be open to change too. Your number 9 might look like a number 6 to your partner, but it doesn't mean your partner is wrong. It simply means you both are looking at the same thing from different perspectives. Couples should try to understand each other, make their points apparent, and then sort out whatever's bothering them.

7. You feel at ease talking about your past:

Our past might be filled with our darkest secrets, but it does, in no way, defines us. When you feel free to tell your partner all about your exes, and the time you got depressed, and any failures or rejections that you received in your past, it shows that you trust your partner completely. Everything that has happened to your history has brought you to where you are today and changed you into a completely different person. Your partner should reassure you, and you shouldn't feel the need to hide any details from them. Similarly, you should comfort your partner and give them the same assurance.

8. You share responsibilities:

A relationship should always be based on equality. Putting the same effort into the success of the relationship is vital. Yes, sometimes your partner may do their 80%, and you have to put in your 120% and vice versa, but being on the same page and sharing all the responsibilities are a significant sign of a healthy relationship. One of you might be over-responsible in certain things, and one of you might be under-responsible in certain things, and it could be the other way around too. The over/under responsible dynamic is natural. However, when it becomes unbalanced, it can set off a cycle of anger, guilt, hurt, and resentment. Making sure of your particular dynamic and working on your responsibilities allows you to grow as an individual and a couple and balance things out.

9. <u>Making your partner feel loved:</u>

You value your partner's emotions and make them feel accepted and important. You ask them about their day, tell them about yours, and listen attentively to whatever they have to say. You both spend quality time together and make memories that you know you'll cherish forever. You never hesitate to try new things with them, maybe go to a restaurant you guys never go to before or go on a spontaneous trip to another city or country. It might be a shared hobby, too, like joining a dance class, jogging daily, or sitting over a cup of coffee. You surprise each other with dates and gifts. And even though the gift might not be that expensive, your partner will hold onto it forever.

10. <u>Your relationship has gotten stronger over time:</u>

The ultimate sign that your relationship is sustainable for the long term is that it only grew stronger with time. No matter how many times your partner has pissed you off or annoyed you, you couldn't help but fall in love with them a little more every day. Your relationship has slowly built, developing deeper roots with each passing year. The great David Foster Wallace once said, "The essential kind of freedom involves attention and awareness and discipline, and being able to care about other people truly and to sacrifice for them over and over in myriad petty, unsexy ways every day."

In conclusion, if you relate to the signs above, consider yourself lucky and cling to your partner for as long as your destiny would allow.

If you found this video helpful, don't forget to like, subscribe, comment, and share this with someone important to you. I hope you learned something valuable today. Take care, have a good rest, and till the next video ☺

Chapter 3:

10 Signs You're Falling In Love

As our Literature master, Shakespeare, once said, 'A heart to love, and in that heart, courage, to make's love known.'

Ah, love! A four-lettered small word that leaves such a heavy impact on people. Falling in love is nothing short of a beautiful experience, but it can also give you a veritable roller-coaster of emotions. From feeling unsure to terrifying, disgusting, exhilarating, and excited, you might feel it all. If your mobile screen pops up and you're hoping to see their name on the screen, or you're looking for their face in a crowd full of thousands, then you, my child, are doomed! You are well familiar with the feeling of getting butterflies just by hearing their voice, the urge to change your wardrobe completely to impress them, the constant need to be with them all the time. It is known that people who are in love tend to care about the other person's needs as they do their own.

You often go out of their way for their happiness. Whether it's something as small as making their favorite dish or impressing them with some grand gestures, you always try to make them feel content and happy.

If you're in the middle of some casual inquiry into whether you're falling in love, then we are here to help you. Below are some signs for you to discover if it's really just simply a loss of appetite or if you're merely lovesick.

1. You don't hesitate to try new things with them:

One of the factors that you could look into is that you become fearless and more adventurous when you are in love. You don't hang back to step out of your comfort zone and engage in all your partner favors' activities and interests. Suddenly the idea of trying sushi or wearing something bright doesn't seem so crazy. You are willing to be more daring and open to new experiences. You are ready to go on that spontaneous trip with them and make memories, all while being a little scared inside. But isn't love all about trying new things with your partner? The New York Times article in 2008 revealed that people in a relationship who try new hobbies together help keep the spark alive long after the honeymoon phase is over.

2. You're always thinking about them:

When you are in love, you always tend to think about your partner. Rehash your last conversation with them, or simply smiling at something they said, or questions like what they must be doing right now, have they eaten their meal yet, did they go to work on time or were late again, are always on the back of your mind. You are mentally, emotionally, and physically impacted about caring for them. But it isn't overwhelming. Instead, you get a sense of a calm and secure reality that you will constantly crave. When in love, we tend to merge with that person in such a way that they start to dominate our thoughts and we become wholly preoccupied with them.

3. You become anxious and stressed:

According to a psychology study, falling in love could also cause higher levels of cortisol, a stress home, in your body. So the next time you feel jittery or anxious, that person might mean more to you than you think. You might become anxious to dress up nicely to impress them, or if they ask you something, the pressure of answering them intellectually can be expected. But suppose you're feeling overly anxious about your partner, like them not texting you back instantly or thinking they might be cheating on you. In that case, it's an indication of insecure attachment, and you might want to work on yourself to avoid feeling like this.

4. **You become inspired and motivated:**

A few days ago, you needed the motivation to get out of bed. And now, the future suddenly seems so bright and full of potential. Your partner inspires you to set up new goals, have a positive attitude, and cheer you from behind while you feel full of energy and chase them. When we are in love, a part of our brain, considered the reward system, releases excess dopamine, and we feel invincible, omnipotent, and daring. Your life becomes significantly better when you're around them.

5. **You become empathetic towards them:**

It's not a secret that you start seeing your partner as an extension of yourself and reciprocate whatever they feel when you fall in love. Suppose they are accepted into their favorite program, or they expect to receive that interview call, or their favorite football team might have lost in the quarters. In that case, you might feel the same excitement, happiness, or distress that your partner does. Becoming empathetic towards your partner means making sacrifices for them, like going to the grocery store because your partner is tired or refueling their tank in the cold so that they don't have to step out. According to an expert, "Your love is growing when you have an increased sense of empathy toward your partner. When they feel sad, you feel sad. When they feel happy, you feel happy. This might mean going out of the way to give them love in the way that they want to receive it, even if it is not the way you would want to receive love."

6. It's just plain easy:

You don't have to put in extra effort, and it doesn't seem to drain your energy. Instead, you feel energized and easy. You can be your complete, authentic self around them. And it always just seems to go with the flow. Even the arguments don't feel much heated as they did in the other relationships. When you're in love, you prioritize your partner over your pride and ego. You don't hesitate to apologize to them and keep your relationship above everything. When you are with your partner, and it doesn't feel like hard work, know that they are the one!

7. You crave their presence:

Some theorists say that we are more drawn to kissing, hugging, and physical touch when we fall in love. Physical closeness releases a burst of the love hormone termed Oxytocin, which helps us feel bonded. Of course, you don't want to come as someone too clingy who is permanently attached to his partner's hip, but knowing where your person is or how their day went is what you should be looking forward to. On the flipside, Corticotrophin is released as part of a stress response when we are away from our partner, which can contribute to anxiety and depression.

8. You feel safe around them:

It takes a lot of courage for people to open up to their partners. If you don't mind being vulnerable around them, or if you've opened up to them about your dark past or addressed your insecurities, and they have listened contently to you and reassured you. You have done vice versa with your partner, then that's just one of the many signs that you both are in love with each other. Long-lasting love gives you a solid ground and a safe space where you can be upset and vulnerable. When we feel an attachment to our partner, our brain releases the hormones vasopressin and Oxytocin, making us feel secure.

9. You want to introduce them to your family and friends:

You just never shut up about your love interest over the family dinner or when hanging out with your friends. They know all about them, from their favorite spot in the city to the color of their eyes, to how much you adore them and want to spend every single minute talking about them. And now all your family members and friends are curious to meet the guy/girl they have been listening about for the past few weeks. You want to introduce them into every aspect of your life and want it to last this time. So, you make perfect arrangements for them to meet your friends and family, and on the other hand, threatens them to behave Infront of him/her.

10. You care about their happiness:

When you put them and their feelings first, that's how you know it's true love. You don't just want happiness for yourself only, but instead wants it in excess measure for your partner. According to marriage researchers at UC Berkeley, " Spouses who love each other stay together longer, be happier, and support each other more effectively than couples who do not love each other compassionately." You want to go out of your way, or do their favorite thing, to see a smile on their face.

Conclusion:

If you relate to the signs above, then you've already been hit by the love cupid. Scientists have discovered that falling in love, is in fact, a real thing. The brain releases Phenylethylamine, a hormone known for creating feelings of infatuation towards your significant other. The mix and match of different hormones released in our body while we are in love are wondrous. If you have gotten lucky and found a special someone for yourself, then cling to them and don't let them go! If you found this video helpful, please like and subscribe to the channel. Also don't forget to share this video with someone who you find might benefit from this topic as well!

Chapter 4:

7 Signs You Have Found A Keeper

Are you looking for Mr. or Mrs. Right? Or do you think you have found the right person, but how can you be sure? Sometimes, we meet someone who seems like the person you would want to spend your whole life with, but during those times, someone is in for a quick hookup. The only partners worth keeping are the ones that give you the positive vibes that you need after a dull and tedious day, the ones that make you feel happy, and your relationship doesn't feel boring at all. Here are signs that you have found a keeper.

1. They inspire you to become a better person:

When we meet someone very kind, helpful and overall a friendly person that person usually inspires us to be better and luckily the world is full of friendly people. Is your partner like this too? Is he warm, kind, and helpful? Does he inspire you to become a better version of yourself? Then you know you have found yourself a keeper. You know you have found the right person when your partner works hard, gives you and his family time, and has his life organized.

2. They are always there:

There are times when we all suffer when things get tough to handle. At times like these, a person always needs support and love to get through the hard times. If your partner is there for you even when you can't defend yourself and they cheer you up, you know that this is a keeper. A perfect partner is someone who knows how to make you laugh even when you are crying, your partner will never believe the things people talk about behind your back, and he would never hesitate to lend you a hand when you need some help.

3. They know you more than yourself:

Sometimes it fascinates us how someone can know us more than we know ourselves; it feels perfect when someone knows how or what we are thinking. If your partner knows what you are feeling without telling them, then they are the one. Does your partner know what you are comfortable with? Can they tell when you feel upset? Do they motivate you to do better and ask you to chase after your dreams? If so, then don't waste more time thinking if this is the right person for you because it is.

4. Your interests are common:

Sure, opposites attract, but too many differences are not usually suitable for someone's relationship. It would help if you had a common interest with your partner, like having common beliefs, values, and religious perspectives. When you agree on these things, your bond will become more robust, and you would find it very easy to live with that person.

5. They are honest with you:

Finding an honest person is a tiring thing to do; many people lie more than twice a day, but how can that affect your relationship? The right one may lie about small things that don't matter that much, like whether the color suits you or not; they may say those things to make you feel good about yourself, but lying about other things like financial status, health, or fidelity can be more serious. A true keeper would never keep these things from you, and they would always be honest with you even if the truth upsets you.

6. They don't feel tired of you:

Although everyone needs some space, even from the person they love the most, he will never get tired of you if he is the one. Your partner will never feel bored with you; on the contrary, your partner will never get tired of looking at you, admiring you, being with you, and above all, love you. When a person is so in love with you that they want to spend every second of their life with you, then you know you have found a keeper.

7. You are a part of their dreams:

Can your partner not even imagine your life without you? Has your partner already planned his future, and you are a big part of it? If so, you know that this one's a keeper. You both have reached a point in your lives where even thinking about living without each other sounds absurd, and then you know that you have found a keeper.

Conclusion:

A keeper is someone that loves, cherishes, and cares for you like no one has ever had. Don't worry if you haven't found your keeper, and it is just a matter of time before you do because, for every one of us, there is someone out there.

Chapter 5:

6 Relationship Goals To Have

We live in a generation where the term "relationship goals" has become a part of the trendy vernacular. It may seem more like a hashtag than anything else, but we all are eager to go into the depth of its meaning. A beautiful photo of a stunning couple having a good time together? Relationship goals. A cute text message sent to a girlfriend from his boyfriend? Relationship goals. A perfect wedding? Relationship goals. All these might seem sweet and enviable and look like an absolute dream, and it doesn't mean that these come off as accessible to them. If you have ever been in a relationship, you would know exactly what I'm saying.

Love is not always fireworks, passion, and butterflies. Relationships are not just date nights, kisses, and cuddles. And love is not that glamorous as it looks on social media. But when you strive to build something together, involving your selflessness, commitment, and even sweat and tears, those are actual relationship goals. Here is a list of what relationship goals you must have with your partner.

1. Always Do New Things Together

Sure, alone time might be great, but together time is where the magic happens too. Avoiding your relationship becoming mundane and a rut, you both should try to do new things together. This could be choosing any vacation spot or having an exciting adventure together. You both should make a list of all the things you want to do with each other and keep adding stuff that might pop later. Tick things off as you go, and you'll never run out of things to do together.

2. Be Each Other's Biggest Supporters

Perhaps one of the best things about being in a relationship is that you'll always have someone in your corner. Regardless of how crazy or unrealistic your dreams and goals may sound, your partner should be your biggest supporter. Seeing the person you love believing in could come off as a massive motivation to achieve your goals. This goes both ways; both men and women need to feel emotionally supported. You both should take some time out to discuss what emotional support looks like to you, what and when you need it, and then provide the said support for each other.

3. Put Each Other First

Putting each other first in your relationship will ensure that you're paying attention to each other's needs and making sure they are being met. You have become selfless with each other, and you both strive to make each other happy and would do anything to put a smile on each other's faces. You complement each other, protect each other, support and love each other, no matter the obstacles or circumstances.

4. Know The Importance of Alone Time

As much as you don't want to keep your hands off your partner in the early stages of your relationship, it's essential to know that you both need time alone to recharge and refill your cup. Spending all of your time together isn't sustainable, and alone time is significant. It will help you maintain your individuality, allow you breathing space, and encourage a closer relationship with each other when you spend time together.

5. Keep The Physical Connection Going

Sex isn't always an option when dealing with different phases of your relationship. There are going to be times when it might not be physically or mentally possible. But this in no way means that you should stop all physical connections. Physically touching the person you love releases an oxytocin hormone; this feel-good love hormone reduces stress and makes you feel wonderful things. You can stay physically connected by holding hands, cuddling, or simply leaning on one another.

6. Speak Positively About Each Other

Speaking ill of your partner with others is not only disrespectful to them, but it's also disrespectful to your relationship. Sure, you can vent in tough times, but make sure you talk about the actions and behaviors that upset you and not their personality traits. Always speak positively and kindly of each other. Even if their behavior irritates you, focus more on the characteristics you love of them and let it pass.

Conclusion

Relationships are complicated but beautiful at the same time. As simple as the above factors may sound to you, these things take a lot of effort and hard work to be implemented. But when you do all of these with the person you love the most in the world, then all of it can be worth it.

Chapter 6:

6 Ways To Make Your Relationship Sweeter

Being in love is the most beautiful thing ever for some of us. Everything seems bright and colorful. You feel happy all the time, and the things you once hated seem good enough to try. However, everything takes time. When you both grow together and get to know each other better, it takes a lot of time. And of course, having strong feelings for each other is necessary for a relationship. A relationship is a way of loving someone openly and keeping someone your priority by your own free will and being someone else's priority too.

Relationships are sweet on their own. There is not much hard work needed when you are naturally and effortlessly in love with each other. Even though there are countless ways, you can dial a notch up and make your relationship even more robust, healthier, and sweeter than before. It takes a lot of time to manage everything, but love is worth it when you are with the right person. All the work and compromises seem worth it. Once you are with your charming prince and your dream princess, everything other than that is just a piece of cake. Following are some ways to make your relationship even sweeter.

1. Go On A date Occasionally

Going on a date with the one that you love is highly romantic and sweet. It's essential to keep that spark alive between the two of you, and a date might be a perfect idea to spend some time together. It is not necessary to go out every time. Cuddling and movies sound like a sweet and comfortable date. It's easier for you to tire out of all the work of the day. A date might give you that energy boost that you need. No matter how long you have been dating, a date is perfect for you.

2. Share Your Day

Going through a hectic schedule is much work on themselves. When we come home to someone who will listen to us rant about every detail of our hectic day, our day gets better somehow. We get a weird sense of comfort to know that there might be someone willing to listen to us every day. The same goes the other way around; you need to listen attentively and remember the details. This shows that you care about your partner and your relationship turns sweeter.

3. Complement Each Other

When you try to look your best, put on your best dress and do on-point make-up. All you need is someone to compliment you on putting that charming smile on your face too. In a relationship, when both people compliment each other, not only does it sound sweet, but it boosts the confidence of the other partner. It would be best to remind your other half that they look perfect no matter how they dress or look because it's the love that matters.

4. Constant "I love you's."

When you randomly tell your partner how much you love them, nothing can be much sweeter than that. Those small moments of saying "I love you" can mean a lot to the other person. It might make their difficult day brighter. It can make them lose all their stress in an instant—elaborate your love. Tell them why you love them. Tell them you make them happy. It makes a relationship much more robust than before.

5. Physical Affection

Showing physical affection to each other sounds so romantic, as romantic as it feels. You were looking into each other's eyes, holding each other's hand and cuddling with each other. These small gestures may sound bland and ordinary. But they can feel like you have conquered the world. These are the feelings that make a bond more assertive and make a relationship sweeter. It would be best if you kept the flirting moving on to keep the spark alive in your relationship.

6. Gifts and Presents

You don't need a special occasion to gift your partner something. Surprise them randomly. It doesn't mean expensive gifts or unaffordable presents. Something sweet and personal will make them happy too. Like making their favorite dish or dessert, buying them their favorite perfume, or gift them something that personally means a lot to both of you. These simple ideas can make their whole day special.

Conclusion:

Maintaining a relationship might not be as easy as it sounds, but when you are with the one you live and love to spend time with, then everything can be bearable. You need to keep the spark alive and keep each other strong individually as well.

Chapter 7:

9 Ways Women Fall In Love

Opening

What makes a woman fall in love with men? Different TV shows and movies portray various scenarios of women falling in love only with rich and handsome guys. Think the Bachelor or some cheesy dating show. As a result we are incline to think that women will only like us if we are rich and handsome as well. But in reality women are far more complex and do see past the money, glamour, and attractive looks, to something that holds more dearly to their heart.

While women fall in love differently than men, they strongly desire their partners to respect, understand, love, and appreciate them for who they are. As a guy, it can be complicated to know the different ways that women fall in love with men. We make this easier for you. In this video, we will share eight different ways that they do just that. Let's get started!

1. She desires to be familiar with you

While this is true for both sexes, women show a greater desire to know their partner through spending quality time and making meaningful memories together. This helps them develop a more profound understanding of a potential soul mate. A woman wants to know if he is the one that she can build a memorable future together. On the contrary, men tend to favor the need to feel attraction in the beginning of a relationship, which I must say is usually mostly physical.

If she desires to be familiar with you, it is a sign that she might be considering you for the part. It is significant to remember that while physical looks are important, your personality and a deep personal and emotional connection is the one that will determine if a woman will fall in love with you.

2. They look for thoughtfulness

Being highly thoughtful themselves, women feel excited and much happier with a thoughtful man. They fancy feeling special, desired, and appreciated a top priority in an ideal partner that can give that to them. Receiving a sweet text message or flowers is extremely romantic for many women. They also truly admire men who remember special dates and occasions. If you can do these things with your eyes closed, you have already won half the battle.

3. She wants to know your Thoughts

Estrogen is known as the female sex hormone and it plays an integral role in remembering special memoirs, comprehending abstract conceptions, and other general webbed thoughts. A woman wants to know that her partner can initiate and understand meaningful or logical perceptions.

While it is wonderful to connect with someone through enjoyable dates and activities, women don't fall in love unless they are attracted to someone's thought-oriented personality. Do we appreciate similar life perspectives? Does he inspire me to advance my life knowledge? Intelligence is the most important aspect of a healthy relationship. A woman does not look for an intelligent partner to answer her questions, but she is particularly interested in discovering momentous life philosophies with her partner.

4. She desires to have a great communicator

Being able to have regular great conversations with a man is something highly sought after in women. Women often fall in love knowing they can engage in healthy communications with their partners. Having a meaningful connection is key here.

Do you know women particularly check the verbal communication skills of their partners to establish a deeper understanding of their personalities? It does not mean women don't appreciate silence, but a good balance between the two is the takeaway here. Women fall in love with guys who participate in good debates that challenge them intellectually without coming across as arrogant.

5. Value for Family

It's highly attractive for women to see a man giving higher consideration to his or her family. A woman truly appreciates a man who takes great care of his family and treats them with due respect. It is an obvious sign that he will give the same amount of respect to her as well. She feels truly grateful when he introduces her to his parents and exerts all his efforts to win the hearts of her family.

While we may not be able to control how family members think and behave, it is the effort and initiative of a man to win their approval that makes them the apple of any woman's eye.

6. She wants to have a trustworthy partner

While it may be controversial to say in this day and age, biologically, women are child-bearers. If having a child is a priority for a woman, they will naturally have a desire to find someone who is proven to be a reliable and trustworthy partner. A partner that will prioritize being a father some day and all that major responsibilities that come with it as a result. A woman will fall in love with a man knowing that they will be able to provide and take care of the family in the future.

If having kids is not a priority, having a trustworthy partner in other areas such as fidelity is also significant for a woman. Knowing she can trust you will be an easy way to win over her heart.

7. She desires to know if she can be herself with you

While it equally applies to both men and women, it does not lessen its significance when a woman determines it before falling in love. Since vulnerability is a widely accepted element in having sincere feelings for someone, a woman wishes to know if you can accept her for who she is without changing anything about her. A woman truly falls for a guy who accepts her the way she is and appreciates her presence in his life.

8. Please be gentle, man

Now last but not least...!

A woman will never give her sincere feelings to someone who is not gentle to her. Having a supportive, loving, caring, and easygoing partner is one of the top elements that women consider while falling in love.

Having a trustworthy and gentle partner to navigate through life's journey is the fundamental priority of every woman.

Closing

So that's it for today's video. What do you think about these ways of women falling in love? Do you know about any others? Let us know in the comments section below. Do not forget to subscribe to our channel, like, and share this video.

Thank you!

Chapter 8:

7 Ways to Become a Good Partner

Intro:

All relationships are unique. Different Experiences, personalities, interests, beliefs and culture tell us about the possibility of hundreds of different types of couples. However, some foundational qualities assure us of a lasting and healthy relationship no matter what kind of two people are involved. Whether you are in a relationship right now or you are single, you know what works for you, and you might be neglecting without even giving it a second thought. So, right now, what you should do is sit back, relax and think about what worked for you and what did not in your past relationships and what was lacking. You can also ask the people around you who are in committed relationships and what worked for them. Although the relationship dynamics of everyone are different, there is always something to learn. We are going to tell you a secret here. For a healthy and long-lasting relationship, you need to work on yourself first. We are going to list down 7 ways in which you can become a good partner.

1. Be Secure Within Yourself:

So often in your twenties, you feel like you are ready for a lasting relationship, but around that time, most people have not figured out what their passions are, or they are not confident enough. If you still have not figured out your outlet through which you will contribute to the world, and you are trying to lay the foundation of a new relationship, new home, chances are your relationship will not last long because you will feel restless all the time. However, once you have figured out your sense of being, it brings you a sense of contentment. It will be easier for you to maintain the balance between your work and your relationship. If you are secure with who you are, people's comments or words will not be able to bring you down. That can be difficult for people for various reasons, but you will have a happy relationship once you can do it.

2. Be Responsible:

You are going to have good days and bad days. There are going to be days where you will wake up sad and grumpy. After the emotion subsides, you should ask yourself what could be the reason for this. You should always take the responsibility of seeing the truth behind your emotion. Was it your partner's behaviour that made you feel left out or like a third wheel? Tell them. If you feel like your partner is taking advantage of your efforts and are working for this relationship as much as you do, talk to them about this. When you are in a relationship like this, these conversations are not always easy, but you need them to create a stronger bond.

3. Be Appreciative:

If you show appreciation for little things, it will strengthen your relationship. It could be as simple as calling them and letting them know when will you be home, making dinner or putting the garbage on the curb. All these little things show that you appreciate their existence in your life and are considerate of their time and feelings.

4. Laugh Together:

When you laugh as a couple, you open yourself up to your partner; this allows you to be vulnerable. When you can laugh at yourself and themselves in each other's presence, it will build trust towards each other that they will not judge, humiliate or capitalize but rather enjoy these small moments with you.

5. Spend Quality Time Together:

If you treat the relationship in your life as a priority, you will want to spend time together. Of course, there will be times when you will be socializing with others, but that will not give you moments of intimacy or bonding. Instead, you need to take time out to be together. You can have dinner at your favourite restaurant, watch a movie, cook dinner together, go hiking or just simply stay at home and watch Netflix and chill.

6.   Be Their Number One Fan:

All of us can achieve amazing things in life, but when our loved ones appreciate us, it gives us a confidence boost when the people we love are standing behind us, supporting us as we work towards our goals. So as a partner, you need to understand your partner's dreams and goals and support them as they strive to achieve their goals, in good times and bad. You should let them know that you are always going to stand with them. When you know you have your partner's support, it is the best feeling in the world. But always remember, it is a two-way street.

7.   Be a Good Listen and Observer:

Suppose you want to be a good partner. In that case, you must understand what annoys them. To do that, you should pay close attention to what they are saying. You need to listen to them and understand what makes them happy, what upsets them, but simultaneously you should be observing how they react in certain situations. What makes them nervous, and what makes them comfortable. You will get to know more about them by observing.

Conclusion:

We listed how you can be a better partner and make your special feel loved, but you should always remember that a relationship is a two-way street, and they should be putting in the same amount of effort. Make sure that your partner has not become lazy in love, and if you think one of you is getting there, you should have some activities that can bring things back on track, but you and your partner should have a mutual understanding.

Chapter 9:

7 Ways To Live Together In Harmony With Your Partner

A harmonious relationship can make a person's life happy and beautiful, but, unfortunately, not all of us are blessed with a harmonious relationship. It is essential to work on your relationship in order to make it work. Creating a harmonious bond between you and your partner can make your relationship more healthy and stable. The dream relationship of everybody is to feel loved, accepted, and respected but to achieve such a relationship, and you need to first work on yourself. You need to make sure that you are doing your best at making your partner feel loved.

Most people nowadays want to find their soulmates, but even when they see their soulmates, they don't have a peaceful relationship; the lack of harmony causes this.

Here are 7 ways to live together in harmony with your partner.

1. Accept Your Partners The Way They Are

The first step to a harmonious relationship is acceptance. It would be best to accept your partners the way they are; distancing them from yourself because of a simple mistake can lead to a toxic relationship. If you choose to love a person and be with them, you need to accept the good and bad in them. As they say that no one is perfect, we all are a work in progress. When you cannot receive your partner the way they are, a harmonious relationship cannot be achieved. It would help if you allowed them to evolve and support them throughout this journey.

2. Be Gentle And Compassionate

When you embody gentleness and compassion, your relationship bond deepens, and there is harmony in the relationship. Instead of jumping to conclusions and reacting dramatically, you need to respond with gentleness and understand your partner's feelings.

Compassion brings grace to a person. To achieve a harmonious relationship, you should give your partner grace to work on themselves, understand, and give them space to evolve and mature. It may take time, but it strengthens a relationship.

3. Expectations Should Be Released

With expectations comes disappointment. Expectations are the unspoken standards you expected your partner to live up to. When your partner does not live up to your expectations, you might feel upset or disappointed, but how can you have such high expectations from your partner about things that are unspoken. Work on letting go of these ideals that the society and your subconscious mind created about how a relationship should be. Release the attachment to situations turning out a specific way. Brace yourself for different outcomes of different situations. Don't expect too much from your partner because your partner, like you, cannot always live up to your expectation.

4. Personal Space In A Relationship

Every human being needs personal space; we often see couples that are always together. It may feel exciting and comforting at first, but everyone needs their personal space to think and function properly. After being with each other with no personal space, one can start feeling suffocated and may behave negatively. It would help if you had time to breathe, to expand, and to look within. To evolve, you need space. Personal space between couples proves that their relationship is healthy and robust.

5. Honesty

Honest communication is not just a factor to achieve a harmonious relationship but also to have any relationship at all. Not being truthful can cause conflicts and problems in a relationship. Moreover, being a liar can be a toxic trait that can cause your partner to end the relationship. But before being honest with your partner, you need to be honest with yourself. Know your true self, explore the good and bad in yourself. Don't hide your mistakes from your partner; instead, be honest and apologize to them before it is too late. Honesty is a crucial factor in achieving a harmonious relationship.

6. Shun Your Ego

Ego and harmony cannot simply go hand in hand; where ego exists, harmony cannot be established. Often by some people, ego is considered a toxic trait. This is the ego that stops a person from apologizing for his mistakes, which can create tension among the couple. The stubbornness to do things your way is caused by ego and can easily result in unwanted scenarios. These are not the components of a healthy relationship. So to establish a harmonious relationship, you should remove ego and learn to compromise a bit. By removing ego, you allow yourself to be more flexible and understanding.

7. Let Go if Unnecessary Emotional Pain

When you keep hurting over old resentments, you convert that pain into toxic feelings that are not good for a relationship. These poisonous feelings can make you make some bad decisions that may result in your partner feeling unsafe around you. This pain can cause you to bury your positives feeling inside. As a result of this, you may feel pessimistic and may exaggerate minor conflicts into something more. A person must let go of this emotional stress and pain. You can let go by going to a therapist or yoga and meditation. Once you have let go of the pain, your heart is now open to a peaceful and harmonious relationship.

To establish a harmonious relationship, you have to accept and understand your partner and work on yourself. Also, work on your radical integrity.

Chapter 10:

6 Tips To Have A Healthy Long Distance Relationship

Who says long-distance relationships don't last? Well, a lot of your friends and family members would be against it, they would discourage it, and will advise you not to take it too seriously as for them, it'll only lead to your heartbreak. Honestly, it's not going to be easy. Long-distance would make most of the things unachievable, it could get complicated at times, and you will find yourself vulnerable, sad, and lonely. However, that extra distance also plays a role in getting both of you closer. Studies have found that long-distance relationships don't differ significantly from geographically close relationships, and even in some cases, it might even be better.

First of all, you should be comforted in knowing that long-distance relationships can succeed. With that in mind, we have combined a list of tips that will keep your long-distance relationship healthy and ensure that it lasts.

Technology Is Your Best Friend

In this age of facetime-ing and texting without paying sky-high rates, long-distance relationships are now easier than ever. You can share the day-to-day minutia with your partner by instantaneously sharing photos, exchanging texts and calls, and skyping one another. It'sIt's much different than writing a letter to your loved one and waiting weeks or months for a response. People in long-distance relationships also rely more heavily on technology to stay connected with each other. This helps them communicate verbally even more than the couples who see each other often, sit in the same room, and do not interact at all. It's essential not just to generalize but to share details with your partner. It would make both of you feel like you've witnessed each other's day.

Be Commited to The Relationship

This implies to everyone involved in relationships, but especially to people who are pursuing long-distance relationships. It's crucial to know that you're committed to only one person and that you love them before wasting your time as well as theirs. If you're choosing to stay in a long-distance relationship, you both must sort out where you both stand in life, what will happen next in your relationship, and that you both work towards a goal. It can be daunting to plan your future around another person, but it can do wonders for you both if we both work it through. Be vocal about your feelings so that the other person doesn't live in darkness about what you want.

Set An End Date

While long-distance love can be magical, but it's only a great thing for a finite time. Eventually, you would crave wanting to be in the same place as your partner. It can be hard to stay apart for a long time. One thing that'll help couples in this drastic time is to schedule a meeting and look forward to it every day. Both must stay equally committed to the relationship and should be on the same page about how long this situation would last. You and your partner's plans should align in eventually living in the same place.

Do Stuff Together, Even Though You're Apart

If you aren't physically in the same place, it doesn't mean you both can't have fun together. You can plan a movie night via skype or cook something together while facetime-ing each other. There are loads of streaming services available that make it easier to binge-watch your favorite shows with your partner. Apart from that, you can also search for some quizzes or games online that will connect both of you and help you find more about each other. You can also raise controversial topics and spark new and exciting conversations to see your partner's stance.

Make Fun Plans For When You Both Will Meet

Indulge into details of what the two of you will do the next time you see each other. Make it a ritual of discussing all of the stuff with your partner that you so eagerly look forward to doing with them. Be it trying new restaurants every day, or picking up a holiday destination, or simply choosing a new hobby to do together. You can also schedule good night video calls in your PJs to create a sense of you going to bed together.

Set Clear Rules and Boundaries

Don'tDon't do anything that you wouldn't expect your partner to do either. Try your best to stay out of situations that might make your partner feel insecure or uncomfortable. You don't have to check in with your partner for every approval, but you should set clear boundaries for the both of you and adhere to them.

Conclusion

It can get lonely and difficult sometimes when dealing with long-distance but know that the fruits, in the end, will be as sweet as heaven. Constantly inject positive energy into your relationship to keep it alive. Be grateful for your partner and be thankful for the fact that there's someone who loves you and whom you love.

Chapter 11:

6 Gestures That Make People Feel Loved

"Actions speak louder than words ', this phrase is commonly used around us, but hardly anyone knows the real meaning of this phrase. This phrase tells us something about love and the importance of a person. Our actions define us. These actions affect the people around us, it speaks to them in words, we can't speak in. Loving someone is not just enough. You need to show your love, and sometimes the smallest of gestures can make you feel more loved than ever. Everyone wants to feel loved and cared about, and if you truly love them, then show your love, even if it is through a straightforward small text saying, "I miss you." Here are a few ways to make people feel loved.

1. Write Them Notes

Waking up to a heartwarming note on your bedside tables makes someone's day. So whenever you want to show someone how much you love them, just leave them a letter or card. It doesn't matter if you write a few words, either thanking them or telling them how strong they are. These actions affect people the most. It makes them feel loved and, beyond all, appreciated. It also shows that you care about making them feel happy. This note or card will bring a bright smile to their lovely faces.

2. Take Their Favourite Food

"The way to a person's heart is through the stomach," a saying that is quite famous in some parts of the world. Who doesn't feel happy when they get to eat their favorite food. So whoever this person is that you want to make feel loved, on your way back from work, stop by at their favorite restaurant, buy their favorite dish and surprise them with it. Firstly, they will feel loved knowing that you remembered their favorite word and secondly, the food, of course. Now you know whenever someone's feeling low, bring them their favorite food, it'll take their minds off the stressful thing, and they would feel thankful for you.

3. Remind Them Of Their Importance

As easy as it sounds, expressing love is a tricky thing to do. There have been times when we all love someone but don't express it because we feel shy and as a result, they don't feel loved. As everyone grows up, it is easy to feel alone in this world, so always remind people around you how important they are. Tell people you love them, I love you is just a three-word sentence, but the meaning it holds is more profound than the ocean, so don't hesitate and make your loved ones feel loved.

4. Surprise Them

Everyone has different hobbies, and some people like makeup. Someone prefers football over everything else. As everyone is interested in other things, we often hear them talk about these things. Sometimes they talk about how they want something, but they are either saving up for it or don't have the time. Surprise them with things they have talked about and feel excited about. This makes that person feel loved and cared about. They know that you listen to them, and this quality is something that not everyone has.

5. Listen To Them

As I said before, listening is a quality that people often look at in others. We all need that one person who will listen to us and won't interrupt us when we tell them about our day. People feel grateful when they remember that there is still someone that will listen to them no matter what.

6. Include Them In Things That Matter To You

We talked about their interests but remembered you are important too, don't forget about yourself in the process and don't we all know the person who cares about us will always want to know about our lives and support your decisions. So please include them in things that are important to you, fill them in on the ongoing drama of your life, and inform them about your decisions before you take a step ahead.

Conclusion:

When you make someone feel loved, you feel happy, and so do they. Isn't it amazing how easily, by following these steps, you can make someone feel loved? So don't hesitate. Go ahead and show them your love because life's too short to stay hesitant.

Chapter 12:

6 Crazy Ways People Have Met Their Soulmates

Dating is an extreme sport, and it gets more challenging when we hear about the trials and tribulations of not finding "the right one." despite how complex the dating world may be, we may see a good partner if we're lucky enough. When it comes to love, people tend to believe in all sorts of things, be it fate, soulmates, luck, or even claim that one looks at a particular person and they were assured that they would spend the rest of their lives with them. Whether you believe in love at first sight or enjoy reading how couples met, here is a list of some crazy ways people have met their soulmates.

1. Love on the high seas:

A lonely swedish sailor named ake viking wrote a letter titled "to someone beautiful and far away" one night. Once he was done, he put it in a bottle and tossed it in the sea, and hoped that fate would help him find the love of his life. As common sense would dictate, the bottle should've been destroyed or washed up adrift on some lonely piece of land. But, two years later, ake received a reply from a young sicilian girl named paolina. The two begin writing letters to each other, and ake decides to move to sicily to be with paolina.

2. Love at first flight:

Marsha bobb had a date with american airlines and walked down her flight from jamaica to miami in 2005. She saw lenny space sitting at her spot on the window seat and didn't like it one bit. She was forced to sit in the open center seat. At first, she was grumpy with the situation, but she realized he was a decent fellow when she talked to lenny. On the other hand, one look at marsha and lenny fell head over heels in love with her. They would chat for hours to no end. They lost touch with one another in the middle but got back and now are married.

3. Facebook plays cupid:

When facebook had all the hype, a man named schuyler benson of arkansas tried to log into the website on his flip phone. The phone glitched, and he accidentally accessed the account of a woman named celeste zendler, who lived in colorado. Poor schuyler had no idea what to do as facebook wouldn't let him log out of the stranger's account. Thankfully, he was able to log out, and he sent celeste a friend request. After the glitch, they both started talking, met in person, and fell in love. The couple got engaged and then got married.

4. A text leads to romance:

Kasey bergh, a divorcee for six years, accidentally sent a text message to a stranger while she was in denver working on a project for nestle-purina and was attempting to connect with other employees. The text was sent to henry glendening, who was stuck in an unhappy relationship and a dead-end job. He didn't ignore the text message but let kasey vent about how frustrated she was to be stuck in denver and unable to work on her project. They hit it off instantly and eventually fell in love and started a relationship.

5. A match made in hospital:

Danny robinson and his mother appeared on a radio show to share his story about being diagnosed with inflammatory kidney disease. And it just happened that ashley mcintyre, who was danny's age, overheard her mother and grandmother talking about the young man's tale. Ashley and danny shared the same blood type, and she decided to donate her kidney to him as she felt compassion for him. Ashley turned out to be the perfect donor, and danny instantly fell in love with her. The two families got very close, and danny started a relationship with ashley.

6. Marching into romance:

College can be a great way to meet the love of your life. A lady was in her college marching band, and the guy was her section leader. One day at a football game, everything clicked, and they started talking more and more. They created a relationship and confessed their love a while later. They independently decided to get married, and seven months later, they did it.

Conclusion:

No matter where in the world you are, if fate has decided to let you meet your soulmate, you do meet your soulmate!

Chapter 13:

7 Ways To Make Your Marriage Sweeter

At the beginning of a marriage, one can feel the excitement and sparks that come from its newness. For example, the butterflies you feel before going on a honeymoon can make you feel surprisingly on top of the world. It is the start of a marriage that makes you feel this way. Everything feels fresh at the beginning of marriage as your partner surprises you and makes you feel special.

But as time goes on, the marriage becomes boring. This can often lead to an end of a marriage if not enough effort is put in; to prevent this, you could always keep your wedding fresh and exciting. Even though now both of you are not the same person you used to be in each other's eyes, you could still maintain that tingly sensation by trying to be more surprising.

Here are seven ways to keep your marriage sweeter.

1. Keep surprising each other:

At the start of every marriage, partners often surprise each other with flowers, gifts, or a surprise date. These surprises cause the other partner to feel beloved. Still, people usually stop shaking their partners with such things as time goes on. By continuing to surprise your partner with gifts, flowers, and sweet notes, you keep your marriage fresh. After a while, you learn about the likes and dislikes of your partner. You can easily use that to your advantage by buying them flowers they like or small presents that make them happy. The happiness caused by these small gestures of love can keep the relationship from becoming dull. So don't let the element of surprise die.

2. Ask them out on a date:

A relationship often begins with a date, and the date makes you feel nervous and excited. Meeting your partner for the first few times can make you want to look the best version of yourself and continue your efforts to look and be the best for your partners. So don't stop the actions. Ask your partner out on a fancy date to make them happy. Even if you are ordering food from outside, you could still light up some candles and set the table with a fancy dinner set. This could make your partner feel special, and the freshness of the marriage doesn't die with time.

3. Try something new together:

Always try to do something new, like watching movies you liked as a teenager or eating something you haven't tried before; it awakens the excitement your partner feels throughout the day. Try going ice skating or skateboarding together as a fun activity, taking time from your adult routine, and going hiking and other activities to have fun together.

4. Speak about your feelings towards them:

Try voicing your thoughts about them. Don't shy away from words and tell them regularly how much they mean to you or how strongly you feel towards them; simple sentences like "i love you" can profoundly affect your partner. Please don't take your partner for granted but make them feel good about themselves and tell them how important they are in your life. This can make them appreciate your presence, and the relationship will remain fresh.

5. Set life goals together:

You and your partner can decide on some goals that you can achieve together as a couple. It can be any goal, as a financial goal, or exploring the world together. You could save money for vacations together. During this journey, you can motivate each other but can still have fun. Moreover, when you work as a team, it will also strengthen your bond.

6. Turn off your phone:

When spending time with each other, try turning off your phone. This will show your partner how important they are to you. Focus on their words and respond actively. Studies show that a relationship can end when you focus more on social media apps than on your partner. Using too many social media apps can distance you from your partner; try spending more time with them than using your mobile phone to reestablish your bond.

7. Greet each other with excitement:

When a relationship begins, we often see couples embracing each other with love and passion even when they met just yesterday. Still, as time passes, couples can be seen greeting each other with just a simple hello or a short hug. Greeting your partner with excitement and enthusiasm can make them long to meet you. They would be excited all day long because of the way you greet them. This can ensure that the excitement of the relationship doesn't die. You can greet them with a warm, comforting hug or simply a few exciting words; saying mushy things can also make them feel loved, like "i missed you" when they come back home from work.

Conclusion:

By following the above ways, you can keep your partner happy and your marriage fresh and exciting.

Chapter 14:

Dealing With Money in Relationships

When two people first get together, they don't know about each other's financial status. The way a person dresses can never tell how much money they have, as you might have seen people dress humbly but have quite a lot of money. On the other hand, some people spend their money on expensive items and clothes but, in reality, are not that rich. For many people, being financially stable is an essential factor in a relationship. As we have heard, many people say that when you love someone, truly money doesn't matter, but some people hold a different point of view.

However, it is entirely understandable that not everyone chooses love over money; for some people, money is a significant factor in life, but that doesn't mean that one should simply end things with their partner because of their low income. You can always encourage them and help them grow. Believing in your partner is an essential factor in every relationship; if your partner is trying to improve their financial status, then you should be there to give them the strength to continue their hard work.

One should always tell the truth about their income; lying will surely gain you some attention, but the person who truly loves you finds about your lie. It will be hard explaining it to them, and worse, it will end in an awkward situation. Money may attract attention, but in the end, the person who loves you will not be so happy with you, taking you for a lier they may end things. Hence, it is best always to be honest.

One should never date someone just because of their high income; you never know what that kind of person is like. Before starting a relationship, the best thing to do is to get to know each other because getting together with someone just because they are financially stable doesn't always end well. Getting together with someone just because of money can lead to a toxic relationship and may even turn into an abusive one. When you date someone for cash, your subconscious mind starts believing that your partner is the one in control, while in reality, both the partners have an equal role.

No one likes debt, but most of us have obligations. Sometimes, these debts are just a minor inconvenience, but other times, the burden is too much for a person to handle alone. So, always be honest about your financial situation, don't feel embarrassed; maybe when you share your case, your partner may also open about something. When you open up about your situation, you and your partner can find a solution together, and you can easily manage your debts and, with time, even get rid of them all.

When two people in a relationship decide to live together, it may be exciting at first, but the bills are always hard to pay. In such a case, you should always discuss these things with your partner about splitting the bill. Sometimes, you can't always divide the bill because your partner may not have told you but may be suffering from a few financial problems. So, it's better to discuss this kind of thing.

If things are coming to an end because of financial reasons, but you love each other and are willing to work it out, one should seek a relationship counselor. A relationship counselor is an expert at resolving such matters. The counselor can help resolve many problems, including debts, different spending habits, etc.

Always discuss your lifestyle choices if one of you has a costly taste, but your partner can't support it. That may become a problem; if such a problem occurs, then the best thing to do is to discuss such matters, as we all know a healthy relationship demands a person to compromise. Always remember that your relationship with this person is for a reason, so don't give up without trying, try to be honest, discuss things with your partner that is bothering you, and you would be well and good to go.

Chapter 15:

8 Signs Someone Misses You

Missing someone can be very painful, almost as if there is something incomplete about your life. You think about them all the time, and the more you try not to think of them, the more you end up doing that. You might find your thoughts wandering and can't seem to focus on anything other than them. You may either find comfort in binge eating or constantly go through their stuff. Well, you're not the only one who might be going through this torture. What if someone is experiencing the same stuff but for you? Here are some signs that tell you someone is missing you.

1. They keep track of your social media:

If they haven't unfriended, unfollowed, or blocked you yet, the chances are that they are still keeping track of you. If you find them constantly reacting to your stories, or liking your pictures the minute you put them up, then they're visiting your profile again and again. They have kept their slot open for making a conversation or giving you a hint to try to make conversation with them.

2. Did they find your replacement yet?

For someone ready to move on, it takes a second to find a replacement. If they haven't found one yet, the chances are that they are still reminiscing over you. They're hoping that you'll reconnect and thus, still pine after you. Even if they're hooking up with someone as a rebound, chances are they're doing everything in their power to forget you but are failing miserably.

3. They reach out to you randomly:

Receiving those drunk late-night texts/calls? They're miserable, and all they want to do is talk to you. If they were out there having the time of their life, they wouldn't even remember you let alone bother to text or call you. If they do, it's obviously because you're on their mind and alcohol just gave them a head start to get in touch with you again.

4. Rousing your jealousy so you would notice them:

Have they suddenly started posting a lot about their new life on social media? Chances are they're most certainly trying hard to make you sit up and take notice of them. If they're hanging out with a lot of people that you've never seen or heard of and having a fantastic time, then they're trying to make you jealous.

5. They throw shade at you:

If they're making snide comments or remarks about you or a new partner, they're still clearly hurt and miss you. They might pass a statement on your outfit or your appearance and lash out at you, trying to make you feel as bad as they do. They may also show disapproval of your new date and point out negative things about them. It's clear that they still haven't moved on and clung to that thin thread of hope.

6. They do things to get your attention:

Do they post stuff that points towards you? Or do they write cute love letters or poems mentioning you? This is a pretty obvious sign that they miss you and want to get back in their life. They might also ask your friends about you and crash those uninvited parties because they want to see you. You might also see them around more than usual.

7. They hoard your stuff:

Are they still keeping your shirt/hoodie and making excuses not to give it even when you have asked them a million times? Or are they keeping even the most useless thing that you might have given them years ago? It's probably because they go through this stuff and relive all the old memories associated with them. They're still not ready to give them up and move on.

8. From the horse's mouth:

The most obvious and straightforward sign that someone misses you? They tell you themself! Some people don't like to play games and do unnecessary things to gain your attention or throw hints and clues at you and wait for you to notice them. They tell you straight away that they miss you and they want to do something about it.

Conclusion:

Now that you have all the signs on your plate, it's up to you whether you want to give them a second chance or move on from all of this. The choice is yours!

Chapter 16:

8 Signs You Were Actually In Love

Falling in love is something some of us might have experienced, but others? They might be new to this feeling, and they might not even know its love. There is no way someone could tell you are in love except for you. Unlike disney princesses, a bird isn't going to come flying and whisper it in your ear. You have to check the facts and feelings in this case. Initially, love will feel very exciting and adventurous, but eventually, you will be settled and calm. Love is a colorful feeling. And here are some ways you can make sure that what you feel towards someone is love.

1. You feel thrilled around them:

When the person you like excites you and makes you feel ecstatic. Then you got it. You are in love with them. But don't be so sure right away; it can be affected by adrenaline rushes in your body. But mostly, it's the feeling of butterflies fluttering in your stomach and doing somersaults. Your excitement is not expected but above average.

2. You want to see them again and again:

Even if they have just left, you always wait to see them again. You wait for the hours where you will see them. If you, by any reason, have to see them daily, then except for getting boring, it gets exciting and interesting day by day. Even though it's not healthy to not let them leave, you must calm down. It is common in love.

3. You always smile around them:

It's hard to stay severe and uptight when someone you love is around. So, whenever they make a conversation with you, you always smile. You visit happily around them, and that makes your mood go up a thousand folds. When you enjoy being around someone, it's natural. Just make sure to keep that jaw in check.

4. You see the good in them:

When we fall in love with someone, all we see is the good in them. Their sound quality becomes the highlight of their personality, and their flaws seem small and irrelevant. You ignore their bad habits because of one good quality they might have because, in love, flaws don't matter. The good always attracts people, and that is what might have tempted you towards them and forward with love with them.

5. Imagining a future with them:

We can't imagine a future with anyone we see and get attracted to. But when you start to imagine a lot with someone, it's apparent that you want to spend it with them. You might want to make them a part of your real life. And it can also happen with a bit of effort and communication. It will work out in the end.

6. You change yourself a little:

Shaping yourself according to someone's need sure sounds unhealthy, but it's a true sign of love. When you do things that they might like and make yourself acknowledged by them, then you want their attention all to yourself. You dress nicely, you put on makeup, and talk more confidently. These are all the basics you do to impress them with your charm and your will to make them fall in love with you.

7. You are overprotected by them:

You have a hawk-like gaze on everyone that watches over your love interest. Especially your same gender. Possessiveness is fine until it becomes extreme. You know all the people who talk to them and ensure that some particular stay away from them. We all understand this level of love, and it is okay to be overprotective of your loved one.

8. You change your priorities:

When you change your sense of style and mindset, it's evident that next in the line is the priority. They come a level higher every time they do the minimum for you. And eventually, you won't even notice, and they are much higher on that list to ignore. That is why keeping them a priority changes many aspects of your life, making you happy for the good.

Conclusion:

Falling in love is harmless and colorful. It's exciting and wholesome. All the words might not be enough to describe it, but it's a good feeling. You have to accept that you are in love with a person and need to do something about it. You need to let them know and believe your feelings, and you never know? They might feel the same.

Chapter 17:

6 Signs Your Love Is One Sided

While some things are better one-sided, like your favorite ice-cream cone that you don't want to share, your high school diary that knows all your enemies and crushes, and a game of solitaire. But a healthy relationship? Now that should be a two-sided situation. Unfortunately, when you're stuck in a one-sided relationship, it becomes easy to fool yourself every day that what you are experiencing is normal, when in reality, it could actually be toxic or even unworthy and loveless.

They could physically be sitting next to you, but you will find yourself being alone because of your emotional needs not being taken care of. Even though you have committed yourself to your partner, there's a fundamental difference between being selfless in love and giving it all without receiving anything at all. It might be possible that you're in denial, but the below signs of your one-sided love are hard to ignore.

1. You're Constantly Second-Guessing Yourself

If you don't get enough reassurance from your partner and constantly wonder if you are pretty enough, or intelligent enough, or funny enough, and always trying to live up to your partner's expectations, then you're definitely in a one-sided relationship. You tend to focus all of your energy and attention on being liked instead of being your true self and nurtured by your partner. It would be best if you always were your authentic self so the people who genuinely deserve you can get attracted to you and get relationships that match the true you.

2. You Apologize More Than Needed

Everyone makes mistakes. We are not some divine creatures who are all perfect and have no flaws. Sometimes you're at fault, sometimes your partner is. But if you end up saying sorry every single time, even if you had no idea about the fight, then maybe take a deeper look at your relationship. You may think that you're saving your relationship by doing this, but trust me, this is a very unhealthy sign. Cori Dixon-Fyle, founder and psychotherapist at Thriving Path, says, "Avoiding conflict results in dismissing your feelings." Solving fights should always be a team approach and not just one person's responsibility.

3. You're Always Making Excuses For Your Partner

Playing defense is excellent, but only on a soccer team. Suppose you are doing it constantly for your partner and justifying their behaviors to your circle of friends, family, and work colleagues. In that case, you're overlooking something that they are most likely seeing. If the people in your life are constantly alarming you, then maybe you should focus on your partner and see where the signs are coming from.

4. You Feel Insecure About Your Relationship

If you are never indeed at ease with your partner and often question the status of your relationship, then it's a clear sign that you are in a one-sided relationship. If you focus more on analyzing yourself, becoming more alluring, and choosing words or outfits that will keep your partner desiring you, then it's a major red flag. To feel unsettled and all-consumed in a relationship is not only exhausting, but it's also sustainable. Feeling constantly depleted in your relationship is also a sign that it's one-sided.

5. You're Giving Too Much

Giving too much and expecting just a little can never work in the long run. Suppose you're the only one in the relationship who makes all the plans. Do all the chores, remember all the important dates and events, consider stopping or making your partner realize that they aren't giving much in the relationship. Often when people give, they have some expectations in the back of their mind that the giving will be returned, but things fall apart when the other person never had those intentions. It's normal for a short while for one partner to carry the load more than the other; all relationships go through such stages, but constantly engaging in it is unhealthy.

6. You're Never Sure About How They Are Feeling

You can't read people's minds, nor are the communications transparent; you may end up overthinking their behaviors towards you and may be confused about how they're truly feeling. This uncertainty would cause you to dismiss your feelings in favor of thinking about them. This connection may be filled with guessing and speculations rather than knowing reality and seeing where they genuinely stand.

Conclusion

The best way to fix a one-sided relationship is to step away and focus on your self-worth and self-growth instead of trying to water a dead plant. You must focus on flourishing your own life instead of shifting your all to your partner. Your mental health should be your priority.

Chapter 18:

What Happens When You Get Bored In A Relationship

Being bored in your relationship can make you feel unpleasant emotions; you would not feel like yourself. You will be more likely to be over things that excited you before, like sex, date night, vacation with your partner, etc. Even if you don't feel like ending things, the lack of satisfaction would be enough to get you frustrated and ready to break up. Due to this boredom, you may feel stuck in a tedious cycle or feel suffocated. There are many things you will notice about yourself when you are bored of your relationship.

Picking unnecessary fights with your partner is one of the signs that you are bored with them. Dr. Binita Amin, a clinical psychologist, says getting into arguments for innocuous reasons might signify you are bored. If you find yourself bickering with your partner for petty reasons, then you may want to step back and assess why. Boredom can efficiently fuel arguments, but disagreements happen in any relationship; the best way is to see if these arguments are indeed caused by boredom.

Your frustration with your relationship causes these arguments. You can always figure out what is exactly causing this boredom, and maybe you can overcome this problem and carry out a healthy relationship.

Sometimes, we all enjoy comfortable silence, but is that silence comfortable anymore, or is it just because you have no more to speak to each other. Silent meals even when you are in a sit-in restaurant, or even if a few words are exchanged, but those words are in safe and predictable confines, then that is a sign that you are bored. To prevent this, you can try strengthening your bond with your partner.

When we first meet a person we like or at the beginning of a relationship, we put our best self forward, we try to be perfect for them, but when a person feels bored, they no longer place any effort into their relationship. They don't bother looking nice for a date night or don't bother waiting for them at the dinner table because we all know such factors lead to a healthy relationship. Being bored in a relationship can lead to an unhealthy period of your life. But if you are putting in the effort, you know that boredom is far away from your relationship and you.

Have you ever wondered about what it would be like to be with someone else? Even when you are in a relationship. If you have, then that is a sign that you have fallen victim to boredom. It is natural for a person to find more than one person attractive but always pay attention to what is the factor that is causing you to daydream about someone else, and it is simply because you are bored with your relationship. Because if that is the case, you need to make your relationship more exciting or talk and discuss matters with your partner.

Many people in this world are happy to be single, as they say, to be free of any commitment but are that the case with you. Do you wish that you were single? Or envying the single status of your friends? If yes, then you need to take a closer look at your relationship; it may turn out that you feel bored with your relationship, that you no longer feel the passion and excitement of the earlier days of your relationship. If you are glad that your partner is busy with something else, then that is a sign that you are bored.

Don't let boredom be the end of your relationship; you can seek help from relationship counselors, or you can sit around and discuss these matters. Together you can always find a solution to every problem. All relationship requires efforts, so put in your step and let your relationship bloom.

Chapter 19:

6 Ways To Deal With Arguments In A Relationship

Arguments are common in all kinds of relationships, be it with your parents, siblings, friends, or partner. Some degree of conflict can even be healthy as it shows that both of the partners are expressing themselves, rather than keeping their emotions fester and everything inside. Fighting consistently can also lead to a problematic relationship where you and your partner wouldn't be at peace. And if handled poorly, it can also become the cause of the downfall of your relationship.

It's normal to argue with your loved ones from time to time, but if the arguing is continuing at an unhealthy pace, or your disagreements are ending up in hostile silence, or worse, a screaming match, then it can take a severe toll on your life and affect it. Learning ways to handle disagreements constructively must be crucial in every relationship. Conflict is inevitable; it's how you deal with it that counts. Here are some of the ways to deal with arguments in a relationship.

1. **Find Out Why You're Arguing In The First Place**

Sometimes we look at the superficial layer of the issue, not the deeper layers that might discover the real reason behind the argument. If you and your partner frequently argue or about the same things, it can be good to evaluate what really is causing the conflict. You should see if the argument is really what you think you're arguing about, or are other factors involved too? Are there other things happening in your relationship that are worrying or frustrating you? You may want to consider other influences too, like, are there any significant changes happening in your life that's putting extra pressure on you? Maybe you're spending less time with your partner, and the cause of your arguments is sometimes unknown. Or perhaps you're both struggling with something that you aren't ready to talk about. Looking at the broader context of your situation and seeing past your emotions can be a great way to get to the bottom of what's going on.

2. Talking It Over

Talking calmly and constructively when you are actually overwhelmed and feeling emotional can be really difficult. It would be best if you gave yourself and your partner some time to cool off before starting the discussion again. It's essential to open up your feelings to your partner and ask them to do the same. If something's bothering you, you can always talk to your partner calmly and understandably rather than keeping it inside and only giving them hints. No one likes a guessing game in a relationship. Being vocal about your issues and hearing about your partner's, and then talking and sorting it out is critical.

3. Try To Start The Discussion Amicably

Don't start bypassing sarcastic or critical comments, mocking them, or aiming them with gun fires. It can only worsen the situation. Your partner may feel like you're insulting them and not respecting their emotions.

Don't take the arguments personally and make it all about yourself. Try to be calm and patient and start by saying something positive like, "I feel like we have been arguing a lot lately; maybe we should discuss what's causing us both trouble and get back to our loving selves." This will not only make your partner feel important but also might end the argument all in all.

4. Try To See Things From Your Partner's Perspective

A conversation is likely to end up being productive if both partners aren't ready to listen to each other. It can be tempting to get your point across, but if you're looking to resolve things, you should take the time to hear about your partner's side too. They might have an entirely different perspective, but you need to understand it if you want to get to the root of what's causing you both to fight. Try to validate each other's feelings by hearing each other and comforting each other.

5. Keep Tabs On Physical Feelings

If the argument is getting too heated, take some time out to calm yourself and then continue once you're both feeling better. Don't pass remarks that you might later regret, or it could make your fight worse. It could end up leaving both of you seriously hurt.

6. Be Prepared to Compromise

Giving ground by both partners is often the only way to resolve a conflict. If both of you stick rigidly to your desired outcome, the fight would never come to an end. Sometimes, an imperfect solution can be better than having no solution at all. To move past things, one or both of the partners must compromise a little.

Conclusion

It can take some time and practice to disagree calmly and constructively and to change the negative behaviors. But if you stick with working together better, it can produce positive changes in your relationship. Forgive yourself and your partner and move on.

Chapter 20:

9 Tips on How To Have A Strong Relationship

Who doesn't want a strong relationship? Everyone wants to have that high-level understanding with their partner that lasts a lifetime. It is scientifically proven that people who are in healthy relationships have less stress and more happiness.

Healthy relationship not only helps us increase our overall feelings of happiness, but stress-reduction also helps us improve our overall quality of physical and mental health that make every-day life more pleasing to go through. Relationships can be in the form of family, work, friendships, and also romantic ones. Depending on the area that matters the most to you at this very point in your life, you can choose to focus on that specific one until you feel you are ready to focus on the next.

If building powerful relationships is a priority of yours as it is mine, then stay with me till the end of this video because we will be discussing **9 Magical** Tips on How To Have A Strong Relationship with whoever you want. Let's Begin.

Number one

Listen to Each Other

This is the first and probably the most important thing that you might want to take note of. Just think, how many arguments have you had that went in the wrong direction just because no one was willing to simply just listen? In order to understand each other's point of view both parties must be willing to open up their ears instead of their mouths first. You need to have the stamina to listen to their side of the story before airing yours.

If you truly want a healthy relationship then the foundations starts with a good listening ear. To listen not only when the other party have problems in their lives, but also when they have a problem with you. Develop a good sense of compassion and empathy in the process.

Bitter thoughts, grudge-holding, and negativity toward the other person only serve to weaken your relationships, not strengthen them. So try to understand each other, let the other person speak, and then sort things out in the best possible way.

Number two
Give Time For The Relationship To Grow

For any relationship to truly blossom, it is important to spend the necessary quality time together. Whether the relationship is with family members, friends, or lovers, it takes energy and effort nonetheless. Any amount of energy you spend on that person will reap its benefits later. Now, I am not saying to drastically change your life or to go on adventures or expensive dates to make your relationship healthy. All you have to do is simply get yourself free for a day or night once a week and do something different together, like having a date night, playing games, cooking and eating, watching movies or whatever you like, just give your best at that time. Be present with them and don't be distracted checking your phone or replying work messages.

Number three
Give Time To Yourself

Now I needed to talk about this one right after the number two. I think a good relationship should be balanced. In the previous point, I talked about spending quality time in relationships, but I also don't mean that you should give all your energy to them or stop doing things that energizes your soul. Don't sacrifice your own hobbies for the sake of others. I agree that you need to take more initiative in relationships but at the same time you need to take care of your own happiness too. So give time to yourself and spend it doing things that fills your soul with happiness and gratefulness. You will feel recharged and fresh as a result when you engage in your relationships.

Number four
Learn To Appreciate Little Things

This point will touch more on the romantic relationship side of things. If you are in a relationship for quite a while then there is a chance that you might get complacent and too comfortable. You might also gradually forget the little things that make the person special. As a result the other person could potentially feel like you may be taking them for granted. To avoid this, you need to start making it a constant reminder to yourself to appreciate the little things your partner does for you. Say "I love you" to them, give cute little gifts, give them surprises and tell them how much they mean to you. You need to show your partner how much you love them so they never feel taken for granted. So yeah, start doing all this and make your bond strong!!

Number five
Learn To Forgive

It is well said, "relationships require a lot of forgiveness". As I mentioned earlier, bitter thoughts and grudge-holding just hurt your relationship in the long run. So if you want a happy relationship then you should learn to forgive. If there is something on your mind that your partner did and you can't forget then sit and talk to them about it and try to come up with a good solution. If any of you makes any mistake, you should forgive them with a smiling face and tell them that these little mistakes can't lessen your love. Work on yourself, make your heart ready for what you see coming and even what you don't see coming, and let things go in the right direction. You need to make your heart learn to forgive, this is the only key.

Number Six
Don't expect your partner to complete you

You should be confident about whatever you have. If you are looking for a healthy relationship then you should not expect your partner to complete you. Sometimes, we expect things from our partners which we lack and it can put a strain on your relationship. What you could do instead is to constantly work on yourself to the point that you feel you truly and rightfully deserving of every good thing that comes your way. That you feel secure and independent at the same time in the relationship. Loving yourself first goes a long way in maintaining a strong and healthy relationship with others.

Number Seven
Ways Of Showing Love

Different people show and receive love in their own unique ways. Understanding how the other party expresses or receives love is the key to building a strong relationship. Some people do it by caring for you while others express it through physical affection like hugs and kisses. If you don't know that the specific love language is between you and the other party then it might cause problems in the long run. To really ensure the other party feels loved you have to express it in the way that they receive the most strongly. Go find out what they are by asking them and then start giving it right away!

Number eight
Be Flexible

If you want a healthy relationship then you have to learn to be flexible as well. Flexible in the face of any changes that might occur in your relationship. It is a known fact that change is the only constant in life. We may never be prepared but we should do our best to adapt to new situations that we may find ourselves in. It is also therefore unrealistic not to expect our relationships to change as time progresses as well. Learn to adapt and grow in this new stage and you will be all the more happier for it.

Number nine
Make Decisions Jointly

A good and healthy relationship requires listening to each others' desires and concerns. While you may not always love to do the things that the other party wants, you should always try to find a compromise that suits both of your needs. Instead of insisting and making decisions all the time, try making decisions together that both of you will find enjoyable. Be it where to hang out, what to eat for a meal, where to go on a trip together, or even what kinds of products to buy for your home, make sure that the other party's points of view is heard so that they don't end up resenting you over the long run.

Chapter 21:

8 Ways To Make The Sex Good

Has your sex life gone stale? Between kids, work, financial pressures, and all the other stressful things, steamy sex may seem like nothing but a fantasy.

Sex isn't just fun, but it's healthy for you too. Every orgasm releases a burst of oxytocin, which instantly improves your mood. Regular rolls in the hay could also improve your heart health, improve your self-esteem, reduce stress and depression, and help you sleep better. As little as only snuggling together underneath the sheets also make you feel closer to your partner and can enhance your sense of intimacy.

If you're stuck in a sexual rut, trust me, you're not alone. While dry spells are expected in any relationship, it's still no consolation for couples experiencing one. The more we get used to someone, the less exciting sex becomes, as familiarity is the death of sex drive. Treating sexual problems is easier now than ever before.

Here are some quick tips to help you reignite the passion your sex life is lacking.

1. Stop Feeling Insecure About Your Body

It really doesn't matter if you haven't lost the baby weight, your specific body parts aren't as high as they used to be, or you have a pimple the size of an egg; it doesn't matter at all. When you're in bed and making love, your partners are not worried about any of your imperfections. To him, you're still the sexiest lady he fell in love with. Besides, it would be best if you understood that his body isn't perfect either. He might have a large belly or a body full of hair. But he doesn't let it get in the way of a good time, and you shouldn't either.

2. Mark A Date

Scheduling sex might sound controlling and not at all fun, but sometimes planning is in order. You book time in your calendar for many things, so why not do the same to prioritize sex? You have to make some room for it and push it forward. Reconnecting with your partner will remind you why you got attracted to him in the first place. Once you have made that sex appointment, the anticipation can be almost as titillating as the event. So, trade some racy texts or leave a sultry voicemail on his cell.

3. Use Lubrication

Often, the vaginal dryness can lead to painful sex, which can, in turn, lead to flagging libido and growing relationship tensions. To avoid any pain during sex or hurting yourself resulting from it, use lubricating liquids and gels. This will make the sex painless and turn on both of you more and more.

4.   Practice Touching

Sex therapists use sensate focus techniques that can help you re-establish physical intimacy without feeling pressured. Many of the self-help books and educational videos offer many variations on such exercises. You can also ask your partner to touch you in a manner that you would like to be touched by them, or ask them how they want to be touched. This will give you an idea of the range of pressure from gentle to firm that you should use.

5.   Try Different Positions

Sometimes, couples get bored by trying the same 2-3 positions over and over again. Searching and trying new positions will definitely spice up your love life. Developing a repertoire of different sexual positions can enhance your experience of lovemaking and add interest and help you overcome problems. For example, when a man enters his partner from behind, the increased stimulation to the G-spot can help a woman reach orgasm faster.

6.   Write Down Your Fantasies

This exercise can help you explore endless possibilities that you think might turn on you and your partner. It could be anything, from reading an erotic book to watching an aroused scene from a movie or TV show that turned you on, you could re-enact them with your partner. Similarly, you could ask your partner about their fantasies and help them fulfill them. This activity is also helpful for people with low desires.

7. Do Kegel Exercises

Both men and women should improve their sexual fitness by exercising their pelvic floor muscles. To do these exercises, tighten the muscle you would use while trying to stop urine in midstream. Hold the contraction for two or three seconds, then release. Repeat 10 times of five sets a day. These exercises can be done anywhere while driving, sitting at your desk, or standing in a check-out line. At home, women may use vaginal weights to add muscle resistance.

8. Try To Relax

Do something soothing and relaxing together before having sex instead of jumping right into it (not that you can't do that), such as playing a game, watching a movie, or having a nice candlelight dinner.

Conclusion

Lack of communication is often what leads to sex droughts in a relationship. Even if you are sexually mismatched, you can get creative and fix those inequities. Stress and busyness of life, among other factors, can also affect sexual intimacy, but there are fruitful ways to overcome setbacks. Don't let fear or embarrassment stop you from trying new stuff. Tap into something simple to get back on track.

Chapter 22:

8 Signs You Have Found Your Soulmate

"People think a soulmate is your perfect fit, and that's what everyone wants. But a true soulmate is a mirror, the person who shows you everything that is holding you back, the person who brings you to your attention so you can change your life." - Elizabeth Gilbert.

Legends say that even before you were born, the name of your spiritual half was determined. The two souls roam around the world to find their significant other. Whenever they find one another, they will unite, and their spirits would become one. But finding our long-lost soulmate isn't as easy as we think it is. Out of 7 billion people, it could take some time to find out our perfect match. However, when we meet them, we'll click with them instantly and just know in our hearts that they are made for us. A soulmate is someone you keep coming back to, no matter the struggles, challenges, obstacles, downfalls, or any of the circumstances. Everything would feel perfect with them. But how do you know if someone is your soulmate? You needn't worry! We have compiled for you below the signs that you may have found your soulmate.

1. They would bring the best in you:

Have your friends called you boring or a party pooper since you have entered adult life? Of course, you blame it all on the fact that you have grown up now and have responsibilities. But there's this one person who tends to bring out the fun and sassy side of yours. You feel so comfortable around them that you're even willing to try new things with them. They make your anxiety and fear go away in the blink of an eye. Be it singing songs loudly in the crowd, trying bungee jumping, or just packing up your bags and moving across the country with them to pursue your goals and dreams, they will strengthen you by supporting your decisions and being there for you.

2. They won't play games with you:

They won't be inconsistent with you, like making you feel special one day and ignoring you completely the next. You won't be questioning his feelings about you or putting yourself in a state of over-thinking. Sure, they won't make grand gestures like showing up at your window holding a guitar at 3 in the morning or putting up a billboard saying how much they love you (although we will happily accept both). Still, they will make you realize your worth in their life by always prioritizing you, making you happy, asking about you throughout the day, and paying close attention to whatever you say.

3. You respect each other's differences:

When starting a new relationship, people tend to avoid or hold back specific thoughts, beliefs, or opinions. This is because, in the game of love, both of the couple's emotions are at stake. They don't speak their mind until and unless they're entirely comfortable with their partner. Your soulmate would always be open to change and respect your opinions and views, even if they disagree. They wouldn't ever implement their beliefs and ideas on you but would instead find comfort in knowing that you both don't have the same set of minds. It's essential to be on the same page with your partner on certain things, like the future, life goals, children, etc., but it's okay to have different moral and political views, as long as you both respect each other and it doesn't hurt the other's sentiments.

4. You forgive each other:

Being soulmates doesn't save you from the wrath of arguments and fights. Every relationship experiences indifference and frustration from time to time. But it is one of the things that makes your bond stronger with your partner. You both would rather sit and try to talk it through or sort it out instead of going to bed angry at each other. And when it comes to forgiving the other, you both would do it in a heartbeat. You wouldn't consider holding the other person guilty and would make unique gestures to try and make it up with them.

5. You give each other space:

Your partner doesn't constantly bug you by texting and calling you every minute. They don't ask you about your whereabouts and don't act overly possessive. And rightly so, you do the same with them. You give each other your space and know that the other person would always be there for you. Even if you have to ask them about some distance, they respect it without complaining. You both trust each other with your whole heart and respect them enough to give them the space they have asked for.

6. You empathize with each other:

If your soulmate tells you about them getting good grades in college, finding their dream job, or getting a promotion, you find yourself being more excited and happier for them than they are. Sometimes, we feel drained out by showing too much empathy to other people and understanding and friendly. But with your soulmate, you don't have to force it out or pretend, and it just comes naturally. Whenever they feel scared or anxious, you're right there with them, protecting them from the world and not leaving their side until you make sure they're okay.

7. You communicate with each other effectively:

They say that communication is essential for any long-lasting relationship. If you aren't communicating well with your partner, you might find yourself in the depths of overthinking the worst-case scenarios. Your partner makes it easy for you to share with them, even if you hadn't done the deed before. You find yourself talking about the tough things, the things that bother you or hurt you, and they comfort and console you reassure you that they will fix it. Similarly, you make sure your partner speaks your mind to you, and you do your best to right your wrongs and clear any of their doubts.

8. You have seen each other's flaws and still loves each other the same:

It isn't easy to accept someone with the habits or traits that you despise. However, you have been your complete and utter authentic version of yourself with them, and they still love you the same. Be it crying loudly while watching an emotional sitcom, binge eating at night, snoring, burping, or just showing them your weak and vulnerable phase when you tend to push everyone away and dress up like a homeless drug addict. They find your quirks cute and accept you with all your imperfections and flaws, and you do the same with them.

Conclusion:

A soulmate is someone who makes you realize your worth and brings out the best in you. They might drive you crazy, ignites your triggers, stirs your passions, but they might also be your most excellent teacher. They would allow you to discover your true self while always being there for you and supporting you all the way.

Chapter 23:

6 Tips To Find The One

Finding someone who matches our criteria can be a difficult task. We always look for a person who is a knight in shining armor. And by time, we make our type. We are finding someone who looks and behaves like our ideal one. We always fantasize about our right one. No matter how hard it may seem to find someone, we should never lose hope. Sharing is always beneficial. And if you trust someone enough to share your life with them, then it's worth the risk to be taken. The person you chose depends upon you only. The advice can only give you an idea, and you have to act on your own.

Now, when looking for someone from scratch can be difficult for many of us. That person can either be the wrong one or the right one. Only time can tell you that. But you both need to grow together to know if you can survive together. And if not, then separation is the only possible way. But if you find the right one, then it will all be good. You have to have faith in yourself. Be your wingman and go after whatever you desire.

1. Be Patient

When looking for someone you want to spend your time with, someone you want to dedicate a part of your life to, you have to devote your time looking for the one. Be patient with everyone you meet so you will get to know them better. They will be more open towards you when you give them time to open. Doing everything fast will leave you confused. Don't only talk with them. Notice their habits, share secrets and trust them. They will be more comfortable around you when they think that you are willing to cooperate.

2. Keep Your Expectations Neutral

When you find someone for you, they can either leave you disappointed or satisfied. That all depends on your expectations. If you wait for prince charming and get a knight, then you will be nothing but uncomfortable with them. Keep them neutral. Try to make sure that you get to know a person before passing your judgment.

3. Introduce Them To Your Friends

The people who love you tend to get along together. The first thing we do after finding a competitor is telling a friend. We usually go for the people our loved one has chosen for us. While finding the one is all you. They can play a part in giving advice, but they can't decide for you. When we see one, we want everyone to get to know them.

4. Don't Be Discouraged

You are 30 and still haven't found anyone worth your time. If so, then don't get discouraged. That love comes to us when we least expect it. You have to keep looking for that one person who will brighten your days and keep you happy. Please don't go looking for it. It will come to you itself and will make you happy.

5. Look Around You

Sometimes our journey of finding the one can be cut short when we see the one by our side—someone who has been our friend or someone who was with us all along. You will feel happier and more comfortable with finding the right person within your friend. It will make things much more manageable. And one day, you will realize that he was the one all this time. Sometimes we can find one in mutual friends. They may be strangers, but you know a little about them already. However, finding the one within your friend can save you a lot of trouble.

6. Keep The Sparks Fresh

Whatever happens, don't let your spark die because it will become the source of your compassion. It will make a path for you to walk on with your ideal one. Keep that passion, that love alive. If there is no spark, then you will live a life without any light. So, make your partner and yourself feel that compassion in your growth.

Conclusion

Finding one can be a difficult job, but once we find them, they can make us the happiest in the world. And if that person is honest with you, then there is nothing more you should need in one. You can always change your partner until you find the one because they are always their ones too. You have to focus on finding your own.

Chapter 24:

6 Signs You Are Ready To Move To The Next Step In A Relationship

If you're dating someone long enough, chances are you might know them well now and are ready to take your relationship to the next level. You both work out well together through all the ups and downs, connect with each other, and make each other's life wonderful. So whether you're thinking about making your relationship official by introducing them to your family and friends, moving in with them, or even getting engaged, it can both be scary and exciting when you think about making the relationship serious and taking that leap of faith.

If you feel that you have a healthy relationship, you can't imagine your life without your partner and are in a good place emotionally, then say no more. Here are some signs to convince you that you should up your game!

1. **You Both Trust Each Other Fully**

Being able to trust someone entirely isn't as easy as it sounds, especially in times like these and the world we're living in right now. The most significant quality one can look for in a partner is how much they value our trust. If you are confident that your partner will always have your back and you can be weak and vulnerable in front of them, maybe you should consider taking the next step. If you have told something to them in confidence and they don't share the information with anyone, and likewise if you do the same, then you both are fortunate.

2. You Support Each Other Through The Good and Bad

Having someone by your side who you know would always support you, no matter what is nothing short of a blessing. Your partner has always comforted and consoled you through the negative phases and cherished and cheered you through the positive ones. Even if they were dealing with their problems, they made sure you were okay first. Most of the time, we tend to emotionally drain out or become frustrated by being there for people. But with your partner, you are always ready to lend a helping hand and even an ear, listen to all of their problems and shortcomings and support them every step of the way.

3. You Both Apologize To Each Other When Needed

One of the major signs of a toxic relationship is when your partner doesn't apologize or take accountability, even if they know they are wrong. These relationships tend to have a dead end. You might have noticed that your partner admits when wrong and apologizes, even if not straight away; they do it sooner or later. They try to sort out the arguments and fights calmly and try to listen to your point of views and opinions too, instead of forcing theirs on you. They make sure that you're okay after the fight and may even make small gestures to make you feel that they are guilty and you are more important than any of the arguments you both get into.

4.   You Give Each Other Space

You both have a level of freedom and independence both within and outside the relationship. You both aren't on each other's throat and nerves every second. You both have different hobbies and passions that you pursue. You both can meet your friends alone or hang out by yourself, without stressing over if your partner would mind. This is a sign of a healthy relationship when you don't keep buzzing your partner with unlimited calls or texts, ask them about their whereabouts, or cling to them all day.

5.   You're On The Same Page With Them

Even if you and your partner don't share the same goals, hobbies, dreams, passions, or even the same views and opinions, you're still on the same page with them about your values and future. For example, both of you have discussed either having children or no children in the future, getting a destination wedding or a simple one, moving out of the city or across the country, or settling in the same spot where you both are right now. Agreeing on the same stuff shows that you both prioritize the same things and are compatible with stepping up your relationship.

6.   You Feel Safe With

One of the signs that your relationship is ready for the next step is the feeling of comfort and security when you are with them. You can be your utter authentic self with them without fearing that they might judge you or dislike you. You have shown all of your sides to them, the good and the bad, and they still love you regardless. They like your quirks and don't get annoyed or irritated by your behavior. You also have accepted your partner's flaws and imperfections and still look at them the same way.

Conclusion

Taking the next big step in a relationship could be confusing and stressful, especially when you find yourself confused and unclear. So if you have found someone worthy of your time and energy, don't let them go. Instead, cling onto them, and make efforts to keep your relationship floating.

Chapter 25:

5 Languages of Love

What is that one element that fills the human heart with great colors? That is love. The essential factors in our life that make us grow as an individual as well as in pairs. No matter where you stand in your life, there is always this one element somehow involved within you. That is human nature to love. The five languages of love are the different ways to express love. People may have their way of loving others, but they will still fall in one of these five categories. Gary Chapman developed these five languages of love in one of his famous books, "The five love languages: the secret to love that lasts."

The essential part of a relationship is communication. Without it, love is incomplete. Gary Chapman made our lives easier by introducing these five ways to show and receive love. He showed us the way towards everlasting love. It teaches us that understanding each other and communicating are the keys to one's heart. It brings in the romantic feeling that one adores. What else would anyone else want? These are the five languages that grow us.

1. **Words Of Encouragement**

We would love to hear sweet and affirmative things all day long. And it's one of the most romantic ways to describe your feelings through words. In a relationship, words mean a lot. Those small "I love you" and "you make me happy" make butterflies flutter in our stomachs. It's no surprise that one may fall in love with you because of this language of love. It's the short and simple formula to keep your other half happy and satisfied. They will always feel comfortable in your words and will give you some of their own. That is why it is said that "choose your words wisely."

2. **Standard Hours**

When your partner wants to spend time with you, it's evident that you will feel adored. Spending quality time with each other is the best way to grow together and bond with each other. It's essential to be there for each other in times of need to feel loved and cared about. It would help if you made them feel your presence. Make eye contact with them. Hold them. They will feel safe and comfortable. Let them know you are there for them. Spend quality time with them any chance you get.

3. **Acts Of Service**

People who think that action speaks louder than words can do acts of service for their partners. Showing little acts of affection like taking care of them is the most romantic feeling ever. They took care of them when they were sick, held them when they needed to, and made coffee for them in the morning. These little actions speak loud. Your partner will feel pampered with this. This love language is all about showing compassion towards each other. Taking care is a type of love language itself. These acts of service go straight to each other's hearts.

4. Physical Touch

Physical affection is one of the love languages that makes a relationship much better. Physical touch doesn't necessarily mean sex, but holding each other's hands, hugging each other when needed, and holding each other. These slight physical affection can make a person feel loved and admired by their partner. This way, you can show just how much you need each other's physical presence in each other's life. It's the intelligent formula to let your corresponding others know that you will always be there for them. Physical touch is as romantic as any other language of love, sometimes even more.

5. Giving and Receiving Presents

Who doesn't want gifts and presents from their partners? Of course, we all do. Giving a personalized present speaks the language of love. Something your partners have wanted for a long time, and you give them that as a gift. That moment of happiness will be worth it.

On the other hand, receiving such kind of treatment is wondrous. When your other half remembers all about your choices and likes and gives you something. You feel loved. It's a love language that is personalized and pampered with passion and love. It would help if you made each other feel as if you know them better even than themselves.

Conclusion

These five languages of love make relationships everlasting. When you take care of each other's needs and priorities, your partner will automatically fall in love with you. These are the ways you can make someone your lifelong partner and love them forever.

Chapter 26:

5 DIFFERENCES BETWEEN

CRUSHING AND FALLING IN LOVE

It can be difficult to know the difference between a crush and love. When you meet someone and you are overcome with feelings, how do you know what they mean? It is fairly common for someone to obsess over a new flame and decide that it must be love when, in fact, it could easily be a crush or infatuation.

The first thing to know is that love is a feeling you have for someone but backed up with an emotional connection. It's deeper than a crush, and you will want good things to happen to the person you love. A crush is an intense obsession with someone based on surface information such as looks, a job, or even the fact that you go to the same coffee shop. Fortunately, you can look at the following fundamental differences between crush vs. Love and determine for yourself which one you have.

1. How long did it take to develop feelings?

One fundamental difference between having a crush and falling in love is how long it takes to develop feelings. When you have a crush on someone, the feelings come on fast. Sometimes it is called "love at first sight." you meet someone, and you are immediately smitten.

When you love someone, you will develop a deeper emotional connection based on mutual respect and shared values. The only way to know that you share a connection is through shared experiences together.

2. Do you put the object of your love/crush up on a pedestal?

Another great factor in helping you determine whether you have a crush or are feeling love (and vice versa) is determining whether you are putting the person up on a pedestal. Is he or she perfect in your eyes? Do you find yourself using superlative adjectives every time you describe him or her? When you have a crush, the other person often appears flawless and the absolute gold standard in relationships.

When you love someone, you don't think in those terms. You love the person for who he or she is, the good and the bad alike. It's more about feeling emotionally safe and connected than it is about being perfect.

3. How jealous are you?

Jealousy is a sure sign of a crush. Feelings of jealousy come from a place of not feeling as though you can trust the object of your affection. You should never have to feel that way, and it is a sure sign that it is a crush and not love. When you love someone, you have established a connection that is founded on trust and respect. You will be less prone to irrational thoughts and concerns because your feelings are deeper and more genuine.

4. Are you attracted to other people?

Do you find yourself keeping your options open? Are you drawn to others as well as your new flame? If you find that this is true, you have a crush. It may be exciting and send butterflies through your insides when you have a crush, but it isn't fulfilling. Love is different. You will not even notice if another person is looking at you, no matter how attractive he or she may be. Love leaves you wanting to share fun times and quiet dinners with your one and only.

5. Do you cancel on friends and blow off prior commitments?

When you have a crush on someone, you might find yourself feeling like you have to cancel plans to be available for the person. This is a result of insecurity because a crush is founded in idealism, not in reality. When you love someone, you will never feel pressured to make choices. Your partner will respect you and want you to keep your commitments, and you will not feel as though you have to sacrifice yourself to keep his or her interest.

When you meet someone and start a relationship, it can be hard to know if what you have is the real thing. It can be a bit of an emotional roller coaster, but it will settle down rather quickly if you are meant to be. Having a crush can be a lot of fun, but it is important to nip it in the bud once it runs its course. Knowing the signs of a crush vs. Love can help you make the right choices and move on with your life.

Chapter 27:

How To Survive a Long Distance

Relationship

Today we're going to talk about a very touchy yet important subject. If you have a partner who's not local, or you know that they are going to move countries some day, you've gotta be prepared for that time to come. You've got to be sure whether you will begin a long distance relationship or whether you will move to that country to be with that person.

For the purpose of this video, I am going to assume that you have already committed to being in a long distance relationship. And as with any commitment, you have got to be willing to make compromises and sacrifices to maintain that relationship.

There are a couple of things that you will have to mentally prepare yourself for if you are in it for the long haul with this person. They could be gone for days, weeks, months, or even years. First of all you have to ask yourself, are you okay with seeing this person only once every few months? Will you be happy if you wont be able to spend majority of the time with the person throughout the year? How will you cope with the distance? Are you okay with not having physical intimacy with the person? Will you be willing to sacrifice your freedom to wait for this person to return? And can you trust this person to be faithful to you as you spend all your time apart?

For me personally, I was committed to a Long distance relationship once before. And it was the hardest thing for me to do. Especially when it came time at the airport for the send off.

Having already known prior that it would happen someday, i still went ahead with the relationship. All was well and all was fun, but time soon caught up with us and before i knew it, it was already time to say goodbye... temporarily at least. I must admit that it was tough... It was tough because we have gotten so used to spending time together physically in the same space for so long, that this sudden transition was all foreign territory to me. Not being able to touch each other, not being able to meet up for meals, not being able to just hang out at the movies, and not to mention the time zone difference. These were all very real challenges. And they were incredible hard especially in the first few months. I cried at the airport, i cried on the drive home, I was incredibly unhappy, and i was not prepared in any capacity whatsoever to feel this way. You never really know how to feel about something until it actually happens to you.

Knowing that the next time we would see each other would be months away, there was no way to know how to feel or act when suddenly it feels like a limb has been chopped off and you are just struggling to find your feet again. I looked to friends for social support and that was the thing that got me through the toughest periods. Sure we could still FaceTime and call and whatever. Especially in this day and age, but it was still tough having a relationship over the computer. It does feel like on some level you're dating virtually. Everything had to change and I had to relearn what it meant to be in a relationship all over again. I wasn't ever a sappy or clingy boyfriend. I know that about myself. But I do have an expectation to meet up maybe once or twice in a week. Now it's once or twice a year. And it's not fun at all.

So now I put that question back to you, after hearing this part of the story, are you willing to put yourself through this? Or would it be easier if you just chose someone who is in the same physical space with you with no plans on leaving town. If you were to ask me, I might actually do it all over again with someone like that.

The next thing that you've got to have to survive a long distance relationship, is to have a strong social support group. A group of friends that you can share your troubles with. People who can empathise with you, and people who can spend time with you in lieu of your partner. You never want to be in a situation where your partner is your entire world, because when they leave, you will most likely crumble. If you relied on them for all your happiness, their sudden absence will certainly leave you devastated. If u do not have a strong support network of friends, i would suggest you think doubly hard about committing to a long distance relationship.

Now comes the most important part, in my opinion, of having a successful long distance relationship. And that is trust. Trust in each other to be faithful, and trust in each other to do the right thing at all times.

I will bring back to my experience with my long distance relationship. To keep things short, after about a year into my LDR, i discovered that my partner had been cheating on me many times over. And my whole world did come crashing down. Having thought that everything was going according to plan up until that point, i was completely blindsided by the avalanche that hit me. It really hit me hard. But I knew that i loved myself more, and so I packed my bags and flew back home from the trip.

Getting over the relationship was relatively easy because i knew there was nothing left there anymore. There was no more trust to come home to. I had no faith in the relationship anymore and it was effectively over for me. It may sound too easy watching this video, but trust me i went through a great deal and I was incredibly happy with my decision. I learned that i was incredibly resilient and that even though things didn't work out the way i had hoped, and even though my vision of the future was changed drastically, it didn't knock me down. And I chose myself first.

So my question that I put to you now is, to what extent do you trust your partner to be faithful to you? Has he or she cheated on you before? Have they always chosen you first? Can you touch your heart and say they will never do anything to hurt you? Or are you too naive like I was to believe that all is well? Because I was incredibly confident at one point that we were making the LDR work beautifully. Until it suddenly didn't. Would you be okay if you found out that your partner was cheating on you secretly overseas while you guys were apart? Would you be paranoid of the things he could do?

115

If you can answer these things honestly, then u might be able to LDR make it work for you. If not, again, do reconsider your relationship now.

For me personally, If you don't know my stance by now, I absolutely do not believe in LDR. Especially if it's a permanent period. If your partner is gone maybe for a 3-6 month work trip. Yeah maybe that's doable, but if they are gone for 5-6 years and if there's a big question mark behind that... I would totally back away. It would be a deal breaker for me.

The thing with relationships is that, I believe it is the physical presence, the physical connection, the physical communication, and the physical touch that keeps two people together. Without any of these things on a regular basis, it is likely that a couple with drift apart on some level... And without these things, one might be tempted to seek comfort and physical intimacy elsewhere if they can't wait another 5 months before they can see you again.

But if your foundation is incredibly strong, if you guys have made a commitment, if you guys trust each other completely, and if you believe that your relationship can weather any storm, then I already think that you know you can handle a long distance relationship. I am simply here to affirm to you what you already know.

But take me as a word of warning that even strong relationships do fail in the face of a long distance relationship. So you have to be prepared to handle anything that comes your way.

I hope I have been able to shed some light into this topic for you.

Take care and I'll see you in the next one.

CPSIA information can be obtained
at www.ICGtesting.com
Printed in the USA
LVHW050354210122
708836LV00015B/782